# Things to Do on a
# Rainy Day
# Project Book

# Things to Do on a
# Rainy Day
# Project Book

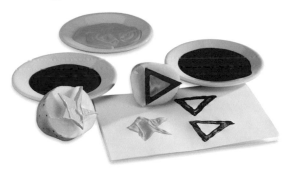

## 50 step-by-step activities
## to keep kids entertained

### Petra Boase

ARMADILLO

## SAFETY NOTE

Crafts and hobbies are great fun to learn and can fill hours of rewarding leisure time, but some points should be remembered for safety and care of the environment.

• Always choose non-toxic materials wherever possible, for example paint, glue and varnishes. Where these are not suitable use materials in a well-ventilated area and always follow manufacturers' instructions.

• Needles, scissors and all sharp tools should be handled with care. Always use a cutting board or mat to avoid damage to surfaces (it is also safer to cut into a firm, hard surface).

• Protect surfaces from paint and glue splashes by laying down old newspapers.

This edition is published by Armadillo,
an imprint of Anness Publishing Ltd, Blaby Road,
Wigston, Leicestershire LE18 4SE; info@anness.com

www.annesspublishing.com

If you like the images in this book and would like to investigate using them for publishing, promotions or advertising, please visit our website www.practicalpictures.com for more information.

Publisher: Joanna Lorenz
Series Editor: Lindsay Porter
Designers: Peter Laws and Lucy Doncaster
Photographer: James Duncan
Stylist: Madeleine Brehaut

### PUBLISHER'S NOTE

Manufacturer: Anness Publishing Ltd, Blaby Road, Wigston,
Leicestershire LE18 4SE, England
For Product Tracking go to: www.annesspublishing.com/tracking
Batch: 6771-22473-1127

# CONTENTS

# INTRODUCTION

It's raining again, and you've read all your books and played with all your toys so what can you do now? Rather than wait for the rain to stop and the sun to shine, why not make some of the exciting projects shown in this book?

Before getting to work on the projects, make sure you read the section on 'Getting Started'. This will tell you how to have fun without making too much mess and having an accident. In some of the projects, such as baking Salt Dough or Potato Printing, you will need the help of an adult.

One of the best parts of making the projects is collecting the materials from around the home. You will be amazed at what you can find. It's a good idea to keep a box for collecting cardboard tubes, cereal boxes, egg cartons, newspaper and plastic bottles. In a short time, you will have collected all sorts of goodies that can be used in the projects.

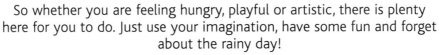

If you find that you do not have all the materials required for a project, make use of those you already have. For example, if you only have a few shades of paint, try mixing them to create different tones. Red and yellow make orange, and blue and yellow make green.

So whether you are feeling hungry, playful or artistic, there is plenty here for you to do. Just use your imagination, have some fun and forget about the rainy day!

# Getting Started

*All the projects in this book can be made easily at home, although some may need adult help. Before you start, read the instructions below to make sure you don't make too much of a mess, and don't have an accident. Remember to ask permission before starting a project and collecting all your materials – you don't want to 'recycle' items that are actually new!*

**Right:** *To prevent your clothes from getting covered in paint and glue, wear a smock or apron, or ask an adult for an old shirt. That way, you can make as much mess as you like!*

**Below:** *When you have decided which projects you are going to make, lay out all the materials you will need on your work surface. You will then find it much easier to get to work.*

**Above:** *If you can find a clear surface to work on, you'll find it much easier to make your projects. If you are using a desk or kitchen table, clear everything away before you begin so you have plenty of room.*

**Below:** *Before you start work on any project, cover the surface you will be working on with newspaper or an old piece of material.*

**Left:** *It is very important to keep all art materials away from your mouth. Not only will they taste very unpleasant, but they could also be dangerous.*

# Materials and Equipment

*These are some of the materials used in the projects in this book. Some you may already have, others you will have to buy.*

**Adhesive tape**
This is a strong tape that can be used for fastening heavy materials.

**Badge pins**
These are glued on to the backs of badges. They can be bought from specialist stores.

**Crêpe and tissue paper sheets**
These come in lots of shades and can be used for making and decorating projects.

**Cress seeds**
These are scattered on moist cotton wool balls and left to grow into cress.

**Dressmaker's pins**
These are used to hold fabric together when sewing. They are very sharp so use them with care.

**Face paints**
These are used for decorating the face and body and can be removed easily with soap or cleansing cream.

**Felt**
This can be used in sewing projects. It is easy to cut and won't go ragged at the edges, unlike normal fabric.

**Felt-tipped pens**
These are always good to use on paper. The shades can't be mixed like paint, so it's best to use them separately.

**Flour**
This is one of the ingredients used for making salt dough.

**Glitter**
This can be glued on to projects as decoration. Place a sheet of paper underneath the project so that any glitter that spills can easily be poured back into the tube once you have finished.

**Paintbrushes**
These are used for applying paint and glue. They should be washed after use.

**Paints**
These must be non-toxic. Different shades can be mixed together to form new ones.

**Paper glue**
This comes in various formats but is easiest to use and least messy when in a tube.

**Pencils and crayons in various shades**
These come in a huge range of shades and should be the non-toxic type.

**Pencil sharpener**
Use this to keep your pencils nice and sharp.

**Pom-poms**
These can be bought from specialist stores or you can make your own. They can be glued or sewn on to projects.

**Rolling pin**
This is used for rolling out salt dough or cookie dough.

**Ruler**
This is used for measuring and for drawing straight lines.

**Safety pin**
This can be used instead of a badge pin.

**Salt**
Use large amounts for the basic salt dough mixture.

**Scissors**
These should not be too sharp and must be handled safely at all times.

**Sewing needle and thread**
These are used to sew with. Needles are very sharp so you must be careful not to hurt yourself. Threads come in a large range of shades.

**White glue**
This must be non-toxic. When undiluted it is very useful for sticking heavy materials together. It can be diluted with water and used for papier-mâché.

*flour*

*salt*

*felt*

*crêpe and tissue paper sheets*

paints

white glue

cress seeds

paintbrushes

rolling pin

scissors

sewing needle
and thread

wax crayons

face paints

safety pin

badge pins

glitter

pencil sharpener

adhesive
tape

paper glue

dressmaker's
pins

ruler

felt-tipped pens

pom-poms

pencils in various shades

# Recyclable Materials

*These materials can be found in or around the house. Always ask permission before using materials such as these in a project.*

**Bark**
Use tree bark as decoration or take rubbings from it.

**Confectionery wrappers**
These can be flattened and smoothed out, then cut into shapes and used as decorations.

**Cork**
This can be used to make your own stamp block.

**Cotton wool ball**
Moisten with water and grow your own cress garden.

**Egg carton**
This can be cut up and used in a papier-mâché project.

**Fabric**
Find scraps around the home and use them in your sewing projects, or use fabric from old clothes.

**Foil**
This can be cut into shapes and used as decoration.

**Foil pie dish**
Fold or cut these up and use as decoration.

**Gravel**
Fill a container with this and use as a musical shaker.

**Ivy**
The leaves can be pressed and used to decorate collages and greeting cards.

**Juice carton**
Use this to make your own periscope.

**Kitchen paper tube**
This can be cut up into whatever size you need.

**Matchbox**
Remove the matches and give them to an adult before using the box.

**Moss**
This is found in a garden. When brought inside it will dry out and fade to a lighter shade.

**Newspaper**
Tear newspaper into pieces and for a papier-mâché project or use it to cover a work surface.

**Paper plates**
Use these as paint palettes or for making masks.

**Pine cones**
These can be turned into tasty bird feeders.

**Plastic cups**
Use these filled with water to wash paintbrushes or for creating models or in projects.

**Raffia**
Use straw as an alternative if you can't find any raffia.

**Scourers**
These are useful out of the kitchen as well as in it, and make good decorations.

**Shells**
These can be painted or left as they are. Always buy shells from a store rather than taking them away from a beach.

**Split bamboo canes**
Use these to help make a beautiful bouquet of flowers.

**Stones**
These come in all shapes and sizes and can be painted and used as paper weights.

**Straws**
Use these for blow-painting or for constructing models.

**String**
Thread beads on to string to make a necklace.

**Terracotta flowerpots**
These may be painted and used to store all kinds of things.

**Tinsel**
Bright and sparkly, tinsel from the Christmas tree can be used as decoration.

**Toothpicks**
These are very useful for making holes in salt dough projects.

plastic cups

cork

pine cones

stone

foil pie dishes

moss

egg carton

juice carton

kitchen
paper tube

split bamboo canes

tinsel

paper plates

bark

foil

terracotta
flowerpots

shells

gravel

cotton wool

fabric

matchbox

string

toothpicks

confectionery
wrappers

ivy

straws

confectionery
cases

scourer

newspaper

raffia

# TECHNIQUES

## Flattening and cutting up a box

*Cardboard can be used for papier-mâché frames among other things. Old boxes are the best source, and you can flatten them out easily.*

**1** Remove any tape from the box and press the cardboard flat.

**2** Cut the cardboard into pieces, ready for use in your projects.

## Re-using foil wrappers

*Foil in various shades is great for decorations, and you don't have to buy it specially. Save pretty confectionery wrappers and cases and cut them into different shapes ready to be stuck on to projects.*

**1** Flatten the wrappers and cases and smooth them out. Cut them up for use in your projects.

## Removing a label from a bottle

*Plastic bottles can be used for all kinds of projects. You should wash them thoroughly before using them and remove any labels.*

**1** Fill a washing-up bowl with some warm water.

**2** Soak the bottle in the water for about ten minutes.

**3** Peel the label off the bottle.

# Papier-mâché

*Papier-mâché can be used for all kinds of things.*
*See the projects for ideas, or make your own designs.*

**YOU WILL NEED**
newspaper
white glue
bowl
water
wooden stick or paintbrush
petroleum jelly (optional)
dressmaker's pin

**1** Tear up sheets of newspaper into small pieces.

**2** For the paste, pour some white glue into a bowl and add water. Mix the two together with a wooden stick or a paintbrush. The mixture should not be too runny.

**3** If you are covering a balloon apply water or petroleum jelly to the surface and a layer of paper. This will stop the shape sticking to the balloon when you burst it.

**5** If you have applied papier-mâché to a balloon, burst the balloon with a pin only when it has thoroughly dried. If necessary, make a small hole and remove the balloon.

**6** If you need to add shapes to your shape, fasten them on with two layers of papier-mâché. Leave them to dry completely before painting the model.

**4** For a balloon mould, apply eight layers of papier-mâché and, for a box, three layers. Paint the surface with the glue mixture and stick on the paper. Leave the papier-mâché to dry in a warm place before painting. This may take 24 hours or longer, depending on the number of layers you have used.

# Salt dough

*Salt dough can be used like clay and baked in the oven until hard. Use this recipe for the salt dough projects in the book.*

**YOU WILL NEED**
300g/11oz/3 cups plain
    (all-purpose) flour
300g/11oz/2 cups,
    plus 30ml/2 tbsp salt
wooden spoon
large bowl
30ml/2 tbsp vegetable oil
200ml/8fl oz/1 cup water

*plain flour*    *salt*

*vegetable oil*

*water*

**1** Put the flour and 300g/11oz/2 cups salt into a large bowl.

**2** Add the oil to the flour and salt mixture and add the remaining salt. Mix all the ingredients together with a large wooden spoon.

**3** Pour in the water and mix thoroughly, making sure there are no lumps.

**4** Knead the dough for about 5 minutes, until it is firm.

**5** When the dough is ready you can use it immediately or store it in an airtight container in the refrigerator.

# Tracing templates

*Some of the projects in this book use templates that you can trace. To transfer the template to another piece of paper, follow these simple instructions.*

**YOU WILL NEED**
tracing paper
pencil
cardboard or paper

**1** Place a piece of tracing paper over the template and draw around the shape using a pencil. The outline should be dark and heavy.

**2** Take the tracing paper off the template and turn it over. Rub over the traced image with a pencil on the reverse side of paper.

**3** Place the tracing on a piece of cardboard or paper with the rubbed pencil side facing down. Draw over the lines you have made with a pencil to transfer the picture.

# Scaling-up

*Sometimes you will want to make a project bigger than the template given in the book. It's easy to make it larger. This is known as scaling-up.*

**1** Draw a box around your original shape. Draw two diagonal lines through the box and to the top edge of the page.

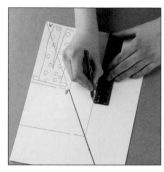

**2** Draw a box as large as you want your scaled-up image to be.

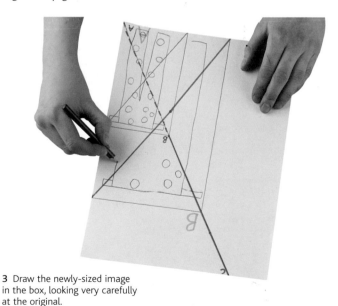

**3** Draw the newly-sized image in the box, looking very carefully at the original.

# TEMPLATES

*These templates are used in some of the projects in the book.*
*You can either trace them directly from the page or make them as large*
*or small as you like, following the instructions given on page 17.*

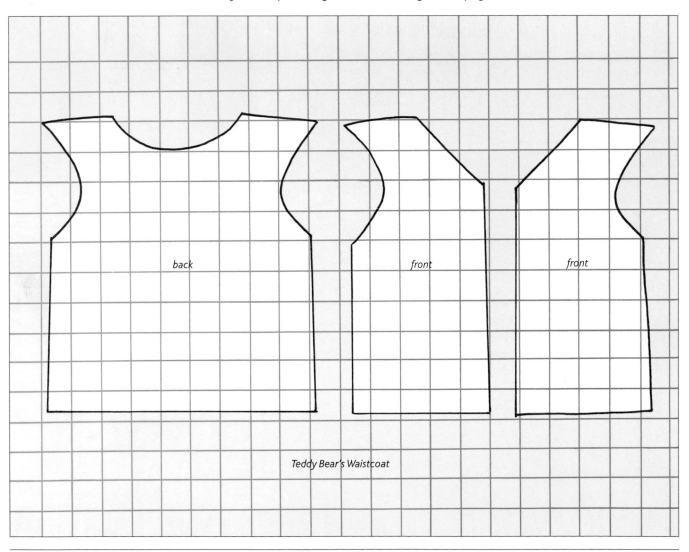

*back*

*front*

*front*

*Teddy Bear's Waistcoat*

*Paper Bead*

*Paper Bead*

*Paper Bead*

*Paper Bead*

*Papier-mâché
Napkin Ring*

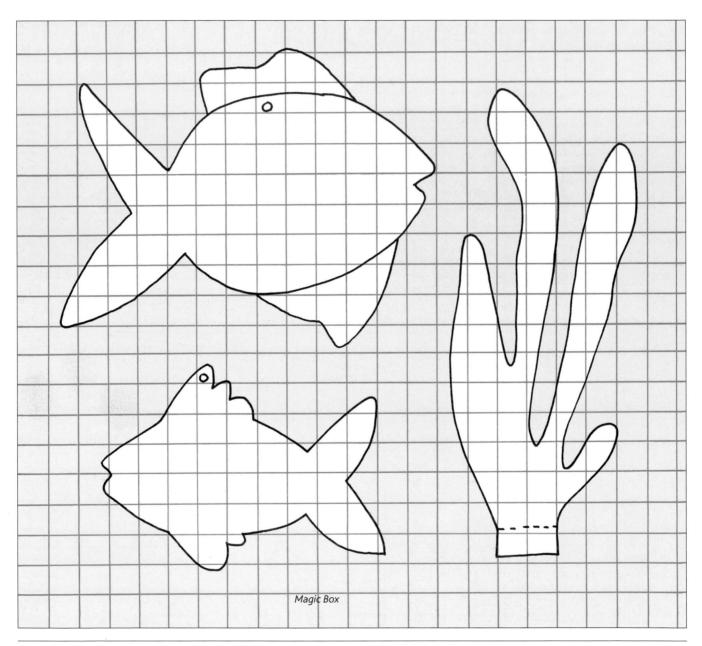

*Magic Box*

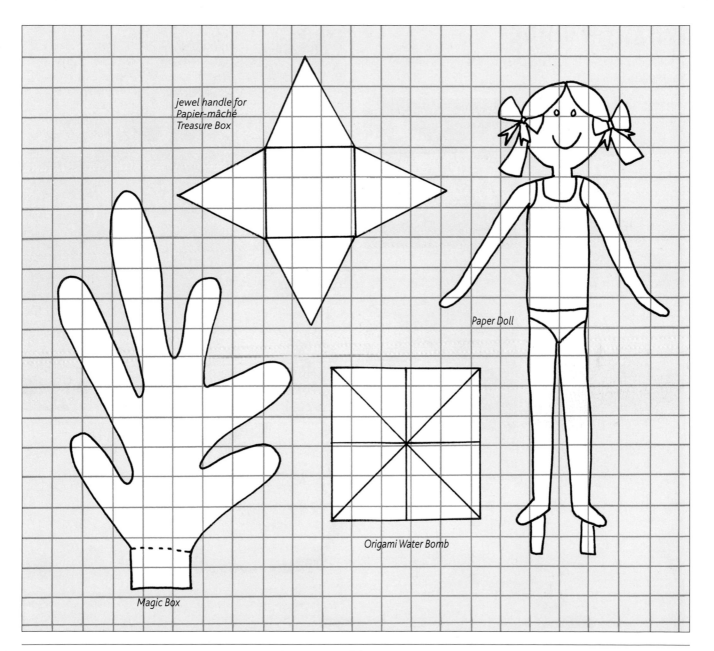

jewel handle for
*Papier-mâché
Treasure Box*

*Paper Doll*

*Origami Water Bomb*

*Magic Box*

## Potato Printing

*Create your own wrapping paper with this simple and fun technique.*

**YOU WILL NEED**
potato
knife
felt-tipped pen
ink in various shades
kitchen paper
paper plate or saucer, for the ink
paper in white or various shades

*paper*

*ink*

*kitchen paper*

*knife*

*paper plate*

*potato*

*felt-tipped pen*

**1** Cut a potato in half with a sharp knife and draw out a shape with a felt-tipped pen.

**2** With the help of an adult, cut out the area around the shape.

**3** Pour a few drops of ink on to a piece of kitchen paper placed on a paper plate or saucer and dab the potato into it.

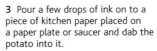

**4** Place the potato on to some paper and press down hard. Repeat this process until the paper is covered with the design.

# String Printing

*Print this string design on tinted paper and cover
your school textbooks.*

**YOU WILL NEED**
cardboard
scissors
white glue
felt-tipped pen
string
saucer or paper plate
paints in various shades
paintbrush
paper in various shades

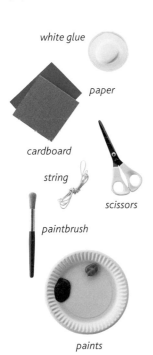

white glue

paper

cardboard

string

scissors

paintbrush

paints

**1** Cut out a few pieces of
cardboard with a pair of scissors
and stick the pieces together with
white glue to make a thick block.

**2** Draw a design on to the
cardboard with the felt-tipped pen.

**3** Cover the cardboard with glue
and stick the string carefully
around the outline of the design.
Allow to dry completely.

**4** Dab paint on to the block with
a paintbrush. Press down on to the
paper. Repeat until the paper is
covered with the design.

# Painting Eggs

*The perfect Easter gift for your friends and family.*
*Put them in baskets or hide them for an egg hunt.*

**YOU WILL NEED**
eggs
dressmaker's pin
small bowl
paints in various shades
paintbrush

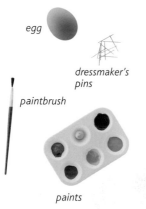

*egg*

*dressmaker's pins*

*paintbrush*

*paints*

1 Carefully pierce a hole in both ends of each egg with a pin. You may need to ask an adult to help you.

2 Carefully blow the contents of the egg into a small bowl. You can the egg for cooking.

3 Paint one half of the egg and leave it to dry. Paint the other half in a different shade if you wish.

4 When the paint is completely dry, add a spotty bow.

5 When the bow is dry, paint a band of different shades around the egg.

6 Finish decorating the egg with bright spots. Repeat as many times as you like to create a whole basket of eggs.

## CRAFT HINT

Make a whole batch of eggs in different shades. You could paint on names or paint faces to look like your friends and family.

# Sponging

*This is a fun and easy way to decorate paper. You could make your own matching cards and wrapping paper.*

**YOU WILL NEED**
cardboard
felt-tipped pen
sharp knife or scissors
paints in various shades
paper plate or saucer
sponge
paper in various shades

*paints*

*sponge*

*felt-tipped pen*

*cardboard*

*paper*

**IMPORTANT SAFETY NOTICE**
You will need an adult to help you cut out the stencil.

**1** Draw the design on to the cardboard with the felt-tipped pen.

**2** Ask an adult to help you cut out the shapes with a sharp knife or scissors.

**3** Put the paints on to a paper plate or saucer, and place the cut-out cardboard on to a piece of paper. Dip the sponge into the first paint shade and dab it on to the paper.

**4** Repeat this process, washing the sponge before using each different shade, until the paper is covered with the design.

# Marbling

*Cover your books and pencil holders with these beautiful marbled prints.*

**YOU WILL NEED**
newspaper
turpentine
oil paints in various shades
plastic cups
wooden stick
washing-up tub or large
  plastic container
cold water
paper

*paper*

*wooden stick*

*oil paints*

**IMPORTANT SAFETY NOTICE**
You will need an adult to help you marble the paper.

1 First of all, cover the work surface with newspaper to avoid too much mess! With an adult's help, pour the turpentine and oil paints into plastic cups and mix well with the stick.

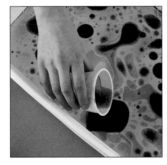

2 Half-fill the washing-up tub or plastic container with cold water. Pour the different paint mixtures into it.

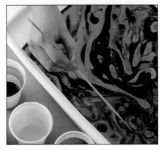

3 Using a stick, stir the paints to make lots of patterns.

4 Carefully place a piece of paper on top of the mixture for 15 seconds then gently remove. Place your prints on top of some newspaper and allow them to dry.

# Painted Terracotta Flowerpots

*Store your odds and ends in these bright pots,*
*or use them to plant bulbs in the spring.*

**YOU WILL NEED**
terracotta flowerpot
paints (acrylic or emulsion)
   in various shades
paintbrushes
varnish (optional)
white glue (optional)

*paints*

*flowerpot*

*varnish*

*paintbrushes*

**1** Paint the inside of the flowerpot in a single shade. Allow to dry.

**2** Paint the outside rim of the pot in another shade. Allow to dry.

**3** Paint the rest of the outside in a third shade.

**4** Paint spots on the inside rim of the pot.

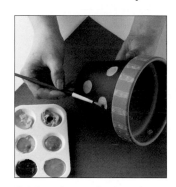

**5** Paint stripes on the rim and spots around the rest of the pot and leave it to dry thoroughly.

**IMPORTANT SAFETY NOTICE**
Always use varnish in an area where there is plenty of air. Do not breathe in the varnish fumes, and clean your brushes throughly afterwards.

**6** Complete the design with more spots. Varnish the pot completely and leave it to dry before using. If you don't want to use varnish, you can use white glue thinned with water. Use a paintbrush to cover the pot. It will dry clear, like varnish.

# Scraper Boards

*Create your own exciting work of art with this fun technique.*
*When you scrape away the background, different shades*
*will appear underneath.*

**YOU WILL NEED**
wax crayons in
   various shades
cardboard
liquid soap
black poster paint
paintbrush
paper clip (fastener)

*paper clips*

*poster paint*

*paintbrush*

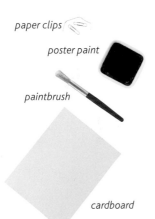

*cardboard*

**1** Rub different wax crayons on to a piece of cardboard until it is completely covered.

**2** Mix a few drops of liquid soap with the black poster paint and paint over the cardboard. Allow to dry.

**3** With an opened-up paper clip, scrape a design on to the card. The bright shades will show through.

# Blow Painting

*You will be amazed at the beautiful shades and wonderful shapes you can create by using this very simple technique.*

**YOU WILL NEED**
paints in various shades
water
plastic cups
paper
straws

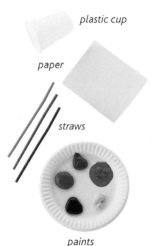

plastic cup

paper

straws

paints

1 Mix each different shade of paint together with water in separate plastic cups.

2 Pour drops of the different paint mixtures on to a piece of paper.

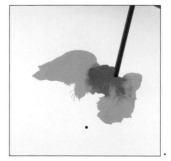

3 Using a straw, carefully blow the paint around the paper to make a striking pattern. Blowing at different speeds will create different results.

4 Add more drops of the paint mixture on to the paper and continue blowing until you are happy with the pattern you have made.

# Making an Exhibition

*Show off your works of art to your friends and family.*
*You can make tickets to allow entry, and make signs for*
*each of the paintings.*

**YOU WILL NEED**
cardboard
pencil
scissors
shiny paper in blue, silver
   and gold
white glue
paintbrushes
glitter
ruler

*cardboard*

*glitter*

*shiny paper*

*white glue*

*paintbrush*

*pencil*

*scissors*

**1** Draw the frame on to a piece of cardboard with a pencil.

**3** Stick the shiny paper on to the cardboard frame with white glue and cut out to match the shape of the cardboard frame. Dab spots of glue around the frame and sprinkle on the glitter.

**2** Carefully cut out the frame with a pair of scissors.

**4** For the exhibition tickets, cut out pieces of cardboard measuring 4 × 8cm (1½ × 3¼in).

**5** Glue silver paper on to the cardboard tickets and cut out gold paper spots. Stick the gold spots on to the silver-covered cardboard. Hang up your paintings and open the exhibition.

# Decorated Stone Paperweight

*Keep your homework under control with this eye-catching paperweight.*

**YOU WILL NEED**
large smooth stone
water
pencil
paints in various shades
paintbrush
felt in various shades
scissors
white glue

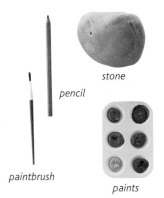

*pencil*

*stone*

*paintbrush*

*paints*

**1** Wash the stone with water and dry it completely before starting to decorate with paints.

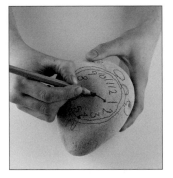

**2** Lightly draw your picture on the stone using a pencil. Here, we have drawn a clock.

**3** Paint the background of the picture on to the stone carefully, then leave to dry.

**4** Paint on the main picture using lots of different paints.

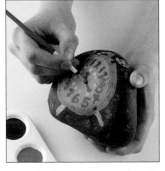

**5** Finish off the painting with small details and leave to dry.

**6** Cut out a piece of bright felt and stick it on to the bottom of the stone with white glue.

# Christmas Stocking

*Hang this stocking at the end of your bed for Santa to fill with plenty of Christmas presents.*

**YOU WILL NEED**
paper
pencil
scissors
bright or patterned fabric
red felt
sewing needle
sewing thread
dressmaker's pins
velvet ribbon
Ric-rac
white glue
paintbrush
buttons

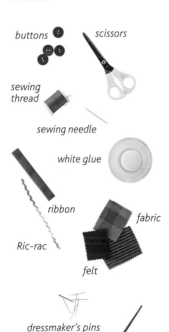

*buttons*

*scissors*

*sewing thread*

*sewing needle*

*white glue*

*ribbon*

*fabric*

*Ric-rac*

*felt*

*dressmaker's pins*

*paintbrush*

**1** Draw a stocking shape on a piece of paper, and use it as a pattern. You will need to make the pattern 1cm (½in) bigger all around to allow for the seam. Cut out two pieces of fabric for the main part of the stocking. Cut out a spiky border from red felt for the top.

**2** Fold over the top edge of each stocking piece and sew with a needle and thread.

**3** Pin the two stocking pieces together making sure the right sides are facing each other. Sew around the bottom and sides leaving a 1cm (½in) seam allowance. Turn the stocking right-side out.

**4** Pin the red spiky felt around the top edge of the stocking together with a piece of velvet ribbon for the loop, and sew.

**5** Stick some more velvet ribbon and some Ric-rac on to the red felt with white glue.

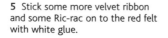

**6** Sew some buttons on to the red felt.

## IMPORTANT SAFETY NOTICE
You may need an adult's help for the sewing. If you don't want to sew, you could make the entire stocking from felt, and glue the sides together with a thin layer of white glue.

# Advent Parcel

*Treat yourself with this parcel filled with plenty of surprises for Christmas. Open one section a day until Christmas by carefully punching open the top.*

**YOU WILL NEED**
4 half-dozen egg cartons
cardboard
white glue
paintbrush
tissue paper sheets in
    various shades
confectionery
crêpe paper sheets in
    various shades
glitter
bright and shiny paper
scissors
paints
ribbon
embroidery thread (floss)

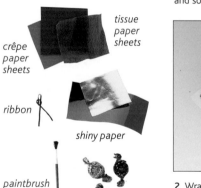

*crêpe paper sheets*

*tissue paper sheets*

*ribbon*

*shiny paper*

*paintbrush*

*confectionery*

*glitter*

*egg carton*

**1** Stick four egg cartons on to a piece of cardboard with white glue. Fill each container with tissue paper and some confectionery.

**2** Wrap up the parcel with bright crêpe paper. Dab spots of glue on to the parcel and carefully sprinkle on the glitter.

**3** Cut out small circles of bright and shiny paper, and stick on the top of each egg compartment. Paint numbers on each circle. Wrap ribbon around the parcel and tie a bow.

**4** Make a gift tag from bright paper and decorate it with some spots of shiny paper. Tie the tag to the bow with a piece of embroidery thread.

# Juggling Squares

*Keep practising your juggling skills and impress everyone around you.*

**YOU WILL NEED**
squares of bright fabric
pencil
ruler
scissors
dressmaker's pins
sewing needle
sewing thread
crumpled paper or newspaper

*fabric*

*sewing needle*   *sewing thread*

*scissors*

*crumpled paper*

*dressmaker's pins*

**IMPORTANT SAFETY NOTICE**
You may need an adult's help for the sewing.

**1** For each juggling square you will need six squares of fabric, 12 × 12cm (4¾ × 4¾in). Cut these out with a pair of scissors. With the right sides facing each other sew the first two squares together with a needle and thread, allowing a 1cm (½in) seam allowance.

**2** Sew all the squares together to form a letter 'T' shape.

**3** Join the sides together to form a cube, leaving one side open for the stuffing. Turn right side out.

**4** Fill the cube with the crumpled paper or newspaper, and, when it is full, sew up the last side.

# Salt Dough Badges and Bedroom Wall Plaque

*Add your own personal style to your bedroom wall and T-shirts.*

**YOU WILL NEED**
salt dough (see page 16)
rolling pin
cardboard, for template
pencil
scissors
knife
baking sheet
oven gloves
spatula
wire rack
paints in various shades
paintbrush
badge pins
white glue

*rolling pin*

*paintbrush*

*badge pins*

*paints*

**1** Make the salt dough following the instructions on page 16. Roll it out on to a surface sprinkled with flour until it is 5mm (¼in) thick. Draw stars and other shapes on to cardboard and cut out. Place the templates on to the dough and cut around them with a knife.

**2** Make some small balls and other decorations out of the dough and stick them to the badges.

**3** Lay the badges out on a greased baking sheet. With the help of an adults, heat the oven to 110°C/ 225°F/Gas ¼ and put in the baking sheet. Cook for 6 hours or until they are hard. Wearing oven gloves, remove the tray from the oven. With a spatula, slide the badges on to a wire rack. Allow to cool before painting.

**4** Paint around the background in bright shades.

**5** Carefully paint the decorations using different shades.

**6** Stick the pins on to the back of the badges with white glue. Leave it to dry before wearing. Make the wall plaque in the same way as you made the badges, but remember to make a hole in the dough before baking so that it can be attached to your door or wall.

## IMPORTANT SAFETY NOTICE
You will need an adult to help you to heat the oven and remove the salt dough once it has been baked. Use oven gloves and do not touch the baking sheet until it has cooled completely.

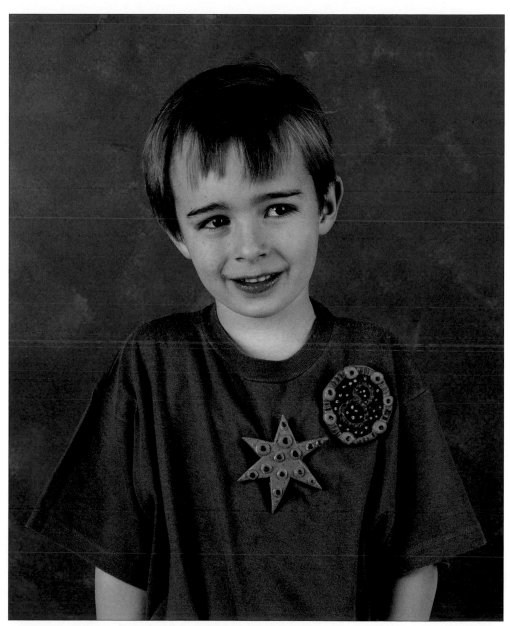

# Make your own Garden

*Create your own indoor garden paradise within a cardboard box. If you use moss from the garden you may need to replace it after a few days if it dries out.*

**YOU WILL NEED**
scissors
ruler
cardboard box
brown paint
paintbrush
small mirror
magazine pictures
odds and ends from the garden
   such as moss, earth, gravel,
   ivy and twigs
shells
non-hardening modelling clay

shells

leaves

gravel

moss

ivy

non-hardening
modelling clay

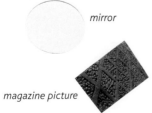

mirror

magazine picture

**1** With a pair of scissors, cut the cardboard box so that it is just 4cm (1½in) deep and paint it brown. Allow to dry.

**2** For the pond, place the mirror in the bottom of the box.

**3** For the garden, arrange the magazine pictures, moss and the shells inside the box around the mirror 'pond'.

**4** For the trees, stick the twigs into a piece of clay and place them among the moss and shells.

**5** Scatter the gravel and earth to cover any bare patches.

**6** Finish off the garden by decorating it with pieces of ivy.

# Blow Soccer

*A fun game for two or more players. Use the blowers to move the ball into the opposite goal.*

**YOU WILL NEED**
pencil
scissors
cardboard or 2 shoe boxes
masking tape
paints in various shades
paintbrush
sticky-back plastic (contact
    paper) in various shades
2 cardboard tubes
Ping-Pong ball
green sticky-back felt

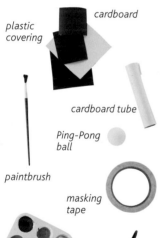

plastic
covering
cardboard
cardboard tube
Ping-Pong
ball
paintbrush
masking
tape
scissors
paints

**1** Draw the goals on to cardboard and cut out with a pair of scissors, or cut one long side off of each shoe box.

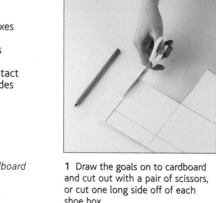

**2** Bend back the two short sides about 2.5cm (1in) so the goal will stand up. Stick the cardboard together with masking tape if necessary.

**3** Paint the goals inside and out. Cut out some spots from the sticky-back plastic and stick them on to the goals.

**4** For the blowers, carefully cover two cardboard tubes with sticky-back plastic.

**5** Paint the Ping-Pong ball with bright paint.

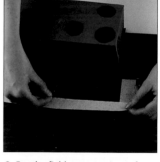

**6** For the field, cover a piece of cardboard as big as you like with green sticky-back felt. Mark out the pitch with masking tape and position the goals.

# Cress Eggs

*These funny eggs have hair that grows. You can give them a haircut and use the 'hair' as a tasty sandwich filling!*

**YOU WILL NEED**
2 eggs
small bowl
cotton wool ball
water
cress seeds
paints in various shades
paintbrush

cress seeds

egg

paintbrush

cotton wool ball

paints

**1** Carefully crack the eggs in half and empty the contents into a small bowl.

**2** Moisten a piece of cotton wool in cold water and place it inside each egg shell half.

**3** Sprinkle a few cress seeds on to the cotton wool. Store the shells in a dark place for two days or until the seeds have sprouted, then transfer to a light area such as a windowsill.

**4** Paint a jolly face on to each egg shell. Cut the cress with scissors when you want to eat it.

# Pine Cone Bird Feeder

*Keep your feathered friends fit and healthy with this tasty meal. You can hang it from a tree outside your window and watch the birds flock to eat.*

**YOU WILL NEED**
large pine cone
peanut butter
knife
bird seed
bowl
string

knife

peanut butter

bird seed

pine cone

string

**1** Begin to fill the pine cone with peanut butter using a knife.

**2** Continue until the cone is completely covered with peanut butter, pushing it into the gaps.

**3** Pour the bird seed into a bowl and dip the peanut butter cone into it, making sure you cover it with seeds.

**4** Tie a piece of string around the bottom of the cone. It is now ready to hang outside for the birds.

# Post Office

*Keep in touch with your friends by running your own post office for letters and packages.*

## YOU WILL NEED
shoe box
masking tape
felt-tipped pen
scissors
paints in various shades
paintbrush
corrugated cardboard
paper in various shades
white glue
string
cork
kitchen paper
jar lid
ink or paint in one shade

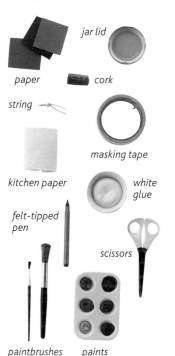

jar lid

paper    cork

string

masking tape

kitchen paper    white glue

felt-tipped pen

scissors

paintbrushes    paints

**1** Stick the lid and shoe box together with masking tape. With a felt-tipped pen, draw a rectangle on the front of the box and cut it out with a pair of scissors. Paint the box all over with blue paint.

**2** Make a jagged-edged decoration and a logo from corrugated cardboard and paper, and stick them on to the front of the box with white glue.

**3** Make envelopes from paper in various shades. Fold in the three sides as shown in the picture above and glue them together.

**4** For the stamps, cut out small squares of paper and stick circles in different shades in the middle of the squares. Draw on a small picture using a felt-tipped pen.

**5** Glue a piece of string around the bottom of the cork to make a pattern.

**6** Put a piece of kitchen paper into a jar lid and pour on a drop of ink or paint. Dab the cork into the ink-filled lid and then print on to the stamp.

# Space Rocket

*Travel in time with your very own rocket, made from objects around the house.*

**YOU WILL NEED**
clear plastic bottle
foil
scourer pad
scissors
double-sided tape
shiny paper
white glue
paintbrush
tinsel
foil pie dishes

*foil pie dish*

*shiny paper*

*adhesive tape*

*scourer pad*

*white glue*

*tinsel*

*scissors*

*plastic bottle*

**1** Fill the bottle with scrunched-up pieces of foil.

**2** Cut the scourer pad in half with a pair of scissors and attach it to the top of the bottle with double-sided tape. Cut out two spots from the shiny paper and stick on to each side of the pad with white glue.

**3** Attach a piece of double-sided tape on to the lid end of the bottle and wrap the tinsel around it.

**4** Cut the pie dishes in half and fold them in half again. Stick to the bottom of the bottle with tape.

**5** Cut out some stars from a piece of shiny paper and stick them on to the bottle with glue or tape.

**6** Cut out two pieces of shiny paper for the wings and glue them on to either side of the bottle.

# Musical Instrument

*Discover your musical talents with this fun, attractive instrument. You can pluck the string and run the stick over the corrugated paper. You can even hit the top or sides like a drum.*

**YOU WILL NEED**
plain and shiny corrugated paper
cardboard box
white glue
felt-tipped pen
scissors
paints in various shades
paintbrush
tinsel
double-sided tape
wooden broom pole
bright adhesive tape
string

white glue

paintbrush

pencil

corrugated paper

string

bright adhesive tape

tinsel

broom pole

scissors

paints

**1** Stick a piece of corrugated paper around the upright sides of the cardboard box with white glue, making sure it is smooth.

**2** With a felt-tipped pen, draw a circle on one side of the box and carefully cut it out with scissors to make a hole.

**3** Glue a piece of shiny corrugated paper on the top of the box. Paint the rest of the box a bright shade of paint.

**4** Stick the tinsel around the hole using either glue or some double-sided tape.

**5** Paint the wooden broom pole and attach it to the side of the box using bright adhesive tape.

**6** Thread the string through the hole at the top of the pole and tie a knot. Make a hole at the top and bottom of the box and thread the string through. Tie a knot to secure. It will need to be very tight to make a noise.

# Periscope

*The easy way to spy and become a secret agent. Hide behind furniture and walls and look over the top without anyone seeing you.*

**YOU WILL NEED**
tall fruit juice or milk carton
paper in a bright shade
white glue
scissors
ruler
pen
2 mirrors
paints in various shades
paintbrush

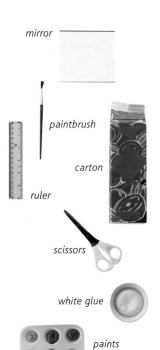

*mirror*

*paintbrush*

*ruler*

*carton*

*scissors*

*white glue*

*paints*

**1** Cover the fruit juice or milk carton in bright paper.

**2** Cut out two holes of the same size at the top of the front of the carton and the bottom of the back with a pair of scissors.

**3** With a ruler, measure and draw two squares on both sides of the carton, level with the holes on the front and back. Divide the squares with a diagonal line. This is to ensure that the mirrors are at the same angle of 45 degrees.

**4** Carefully cut a slit along each diagonal line big enough to slide the mirrors through.

**5** Slip the mirrors in place with the reflecting sides facing each other.

**6** Decorate your finished periscope with painted spots. To use the periscope, look through the bottom hole at the back.

# PAPER PROJECTS

## Matchbox Theatre

*This must be the smallest theatre in the world – you can almost carry it in your pocket.*

**YOU WILL NEED**
kitchen matchbox
scissors
paints in various shades
paintbrush
paper in a bright shade
felt-tipped pen
bright adhesive tape

*paints*

*kitchen matchbox*

*paintbrush*

*scissors*

*bright adhesive tape*

*paper*

**1** Remove the matches from the box and give them to an adult. Take the matchbox apart and cut one-third off the sleeve with a pair of scissors. Paint both the sleeve and tray and leave them to dry before putting them back together.

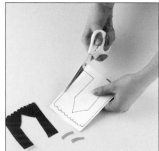

**2** Draw the curtains on a piece of bright paper with a felt-tipped pen and cut them out.

**3** Carefully attach the curtains to the matchbox using bright adhesive tape.

**4** Paint faces on the palm side of your middle and index fingers. Wiggle them inside the theatre.

# Paper Plate Tennis

*A fun game for two or more players to play around the house or outdoors.*

**YOU WILL NEED**
4 paper plates
paints in various shades
paintbrush
scissors
bright adhesive tape
Ping-Pong ball

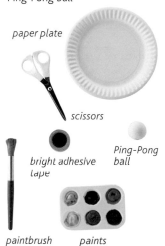

paper plate

scissors

bright adhesive tape

Ping-Pong ball

paintbrush     paints

**1** For each 'racquet' you will need two paper plates. Paint each plate a plain shade. Allow to dry.

**2** Paint patterns, such as stripes and dots or stars as shown here, on to the plates and leave to dry.

**3** Attach the plates with pieces of bright tape, leaving a gap big enough for your hand to slide in.

**4** Paint the Ping-Pong ball a bright shade so you can see it easily. Now you are ready to start playing.

# Papier-mâché Treasure Box

*Keep your precious treasures hidden away in this box.*

**YOU WILL NEED**
small cardboard box
pencil
scissors
cardboard
white glue
paintbrush
tracing and plain paper,
    for template
cardboard
masking tape
water
large bowl
newspaper
wooden stick
paints in various shades
foil confectionery wrappers

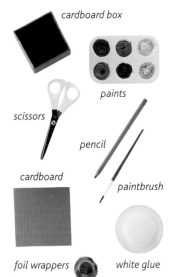

*cardboard box*

*paints*

*scissors*

*pencil*

*cardboard*

*paintbrush*

*foil wrappers*     *white glue*

*newspaper*

*masking tape*

**1** For the lid, draw round the box with a pencil on a piece of cardboard and carefully cut it out with a pair of scissors. Cut out a slightly smaller piece of cardboard and stick this on to the slightly larger piece with white glue. Leave to dry completely.

**2** Trace the jewel template from the beginning of the book following the instructions on page 17. Place this template on to the cardboard

and cut it out. Bend along the marked lines to join the jewel together and fasten securely with masking tape.

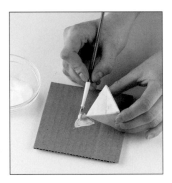

**3** Glue one of the jewel's triangular sides on to the lid.

**4** For the papier-mâché, mix some glue with water in a large bowl and stir in several layers of torn-up newspaper with a wooden stick. Apply three layers of papier-mâché to the box and the lid and allow them to dry overnight in a warm place. (This may take a little longer depending on the time of year.)

**5** When the box is completely dry, paint the inside and the outside of both the box and the lid. Allow the paint to dry.

**6** Flatten the confectionery wrappers and cut out circles from them. Glue the circles on to the box as decoration.

# Papier-mâché Piggy Bank

*You won't find a friendlier pig to look after your pocket money!*

**YOU WILL NEED**
white glue
water
petroleum jelly (optional)
large bowl
newspaper
wooden stick
balloon
dressmaker's pin
egg carton
scissors
masking tape
paints in various shades
paintbrush

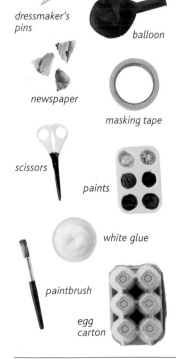

*dressmaker's pins*

*balloon*

*newspaper*

*masking tape*

*scissors*

*paints*

*white glue*

*paintbrush*

*egg carton*

**1** For the papier-mâché, mix some white glue with water in a large mixing bowl and stir in several layers of torn-up newspaper with a stick. Blow up the balloon and tie a knot in it. Cover the balloon with water or petroleum jelly and apply a layer of newspaper, then apply five layers of papier-mâché. Leave to dry overnight in a warm place. (This may take a little longer when the weather is cold.)

**2** Once the papier-mâché is completely dry, burst the balloon with a pin and remove it. You may need to make a small hole to take out the balloon. For the feet and snout, cut up an egg carton with a pair of scissors, dividing up the egg tray and attaching the parts on to the balloon with masking tape.

**3** Cut out triangles from the egg carton for the ears and attach them to the balloon with masking tape. Use papier-mâché to cover over the feet, snout and ears.

**4** For the tail, roll up a piece of newspaper and apply glue to secure it. Wrap the strip around your finger and let go. It should now have a coil shape. Attach it to the balloon with strips of papier-mâché.

**5** When all the papier-mâché is completely dry, apply two coats of paint to the pig.

**6** Cut out the money slot and finish painting the details on to the pig.

# Paper Beads

*These fun and bright beads are made from the pages of a magazine, but no one will guess when you wear them.*

**YOU WILL NEED**
tracing and plain paper,
   for templates
felt-tipped pen
scissors
pictures from magazines
white glue
wooden stick or knitting needle
embroidery thread (floss)

*white glue*

*magazine picture*

*wooden stick*

*thread*

*paintbrush*

*scissors*

**1** Trace the templates from the beginning of the book following the instructions on page 17. Place the templates on to the magazine pictures and draw around them.

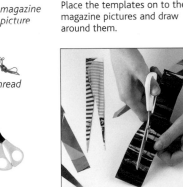

**2** Cut out the shapes with scissors.

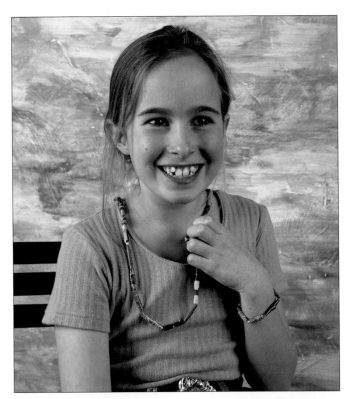

**3** Paint a line of white glue in the middle of the shapes and wrap them tightly around a wooden stick or a knitting needle. Carefully remove the stick or knitting needle.

**4** When the glue has dried completely, thread the beads on to a piece of embroidery thread to make either a necklace or a bracelet and tie a knot.

# Papier-mâché Napkin Ring

*Add some flair to the dinner table with fun napkin rings.*
*You can make your own designs for different occasions.*

## YOU WILL NEED

tracing and plain paper,
  for template
pencil
scissors
cardboard
white glue
cardboard toilet roll inner
masking tape
water
large bowl
newspaper
wooden stick
paints in various shades
paintbrush

cardboard        newspaper

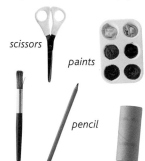
scissors        paints

paintbrush        pencil

white glue        cardboard toilet roll inner

masking tape

**1** Trace the confectionery template from the beginning of the book following the instructions on page 17. Place the template on to the cardboard and cut it out. Stick the confectionery together with white glue. Do not stick the tags because they have to be bent outwards.

**2** Cut a toilet roll inner in half and attach the confectionery to it with masking tape.

**3** For the papier-mâché, mix some glue with water in a large bowl and stir in several layers of torn-up newspaper with a wooden stick. Cover the napkin ring with three layers of papier-mâché and leave to dry overnight in a warm place, until completely dry.

**4** When completely dry, paint the napkin ring in an assortment of shades and patterns.

# Painting Book

*Build up a collection of your paintings and drawings in this cheerful book.*

## YOU WILL NEED
paper in various shades
ruler
pencil
scissors
sewing needle
sewing thread
scraps of fabric
white glue
paints in various shades
paintbrush

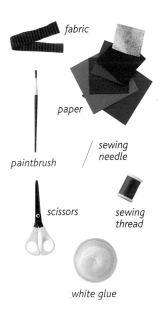

fabric

paper

paintbrush

sewing
needle

scissors

sewing
thread

white glue

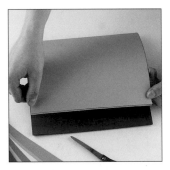

**1** For the pages of the book, cut out eight pieces of bright paper measuring 20 × 40cm (8 × 16in). Divide the paper into two piles of four pages and fold them in half as neatly as you can.

**2** Ask an adult to help you sew the first pack of paper together along the middle fold with a needle and thread.

**3** Sew the first pack to the second pack along the middle fold.

**4** Cut out three strips from the scraps of fabric and stick them on to the two packs of paper with the white glue. This will attach them together securely.

**5** For the cover of the book, fold a piece of bright paper measuring 22 × 44cm (8¾ × 17½in) in half. Glue this on to the front and back of the pack of paper. Leave to dry.

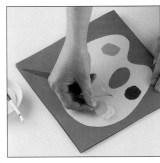

**6** Decorate the cover with a paper collage or drawing.

## IMPORTANT SAFETY NOTICE
You will need an adult's help to sew the pages of the book in steps 2 and 3.

# Origami Water Bomb

*Seek revenge outdoors with this crafty piece of paper work, but be sure to clear up afterwards!*

**YOU WILL NEED**
pencil
ruler
paper in various shades
scissors
water

*paper in various shades*

*scissors*

*water*

*ruler*

**1** Measure a piece of paper 20 × 20cm (8 × 8in). Cut it out with a pair of scissors. Draw lines across the square following the template at the beginning of the book and fold along them to make creases. Take the two creases either side of the square and pinch them into the middle. Press flat to form a neat triangle.

**2** Fold back the corners of the triangle on both sides to form a square shape.

**3** Turn the side corners of the square into the middle. Turn it over and do the same again. Turn the top points into the slots. Turn it over and do the same again.

**4** At one end of the bomb there is a small hole. Blow into it hard to make a cube. Through the hole, fill the bomb with water and you are ready to have some outdoor fun!

# Origami Basket

*Fill this basket with a tasty snack and start munching!*

**YOU WILL NEED**
paper in various shades
scissors
paints in various shades
paintbrush

*paintbrush*

*paints*

*paper*

**1** Cut out a rectangular piece of paper with a pair of scissors. Divide the paper into 16 squares and fold along the lines to make creases. Fold the short sides to the middle crease of the rectangle.

**2** Fold in the four corners as far as the first crease.

**3** Fold back the two middle strips over the four triangles.

**4** Hold the bowl at the middle points and pull the sides up, then apart. Pinch the corner and bottom creases to straighten them. Paint on your own design.

# Paper Flowers

*Make your own everlasting blooms. You could use them to decorate gift-wrapped presents or to brighten up a room in a bright container.*

**YOU WILL NEED**
pencil
bright crêpe paper sheets
scissors
split bamboo canes
green adhesive tape
non-hardening modelling clay

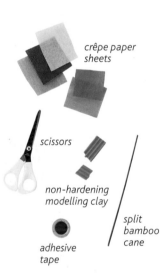

*crêpe paper sheets*

*scissors*

*non-hardening modelling clay*

*split bamboo cane*

*adhesive tape*

**1** With a pencil, draw an assortment of different-sized petal shapes on to bright crêpe paper sheets. Cut them out with a pair of scissors.

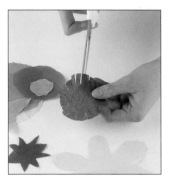

**2** Snip around the edge of one of the petal shapes with scissors to make a fringe.

**3** Starting with the largest petal at the bottom, layer the petals on top of each other, piercing a hole through them carefully with a split bamboo cane.

**4** When all the petals are in place, pinch them together and secure with green adhesive tape.

**5** Roll a piece of clay into a ball and place it in the middle of the cane to make the middle of the flower.

**6** Fan out the petals to finish off. Make more flowers in the same way and place them in a vase.

# Jigsaw Puzzle

*Challenge your family and friends with this home-made jigsaw puzzle.*

**YOU WILL NEED**
vibrant picture or large
    photograph of your choice
cardboard
white glue
scissors
pencil
paintbrush

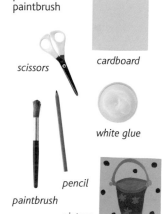

*scissors*

*cardboard*

*white glue*

*paintbrush*

*pencil*

*picture*

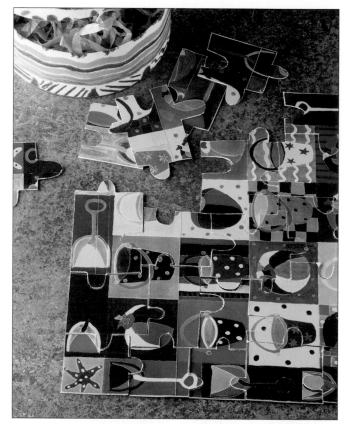

**1** Stick your picture on to a piece of cardboard with white glue. Rub the palm of your hand over the picture to make sure it is completely smooth. Allow it to dry.

**2** Cut around the picture with a pair of scissors to remove the excess cardboard.

## CRAFT HINT
You could cut out a picture from a magazine rather than using a photograph, if you prefer.

**3** Draw the jigsaw pieces on to the reverse of the picture with a pencil.

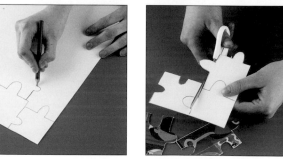

**4** Cut out the jigsaw shapes and keep them in a safe place.

# Paper Doll

*You can create all kinds of outfits for this little doll.*
*Make some friends and family for her to play with,*
*or even some pets.*

## YOU WILL NEED

tracing and plain paper,
   for template
pencil
cardboard
scissors
white paper
paints in various shades
paintbrush
shoe box

*paints*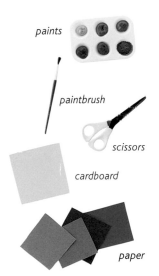

*paintbrush*

*scissors*

*cardboard*

*paper*

**1** For the doll, scale up the template from the beginning of the book following the instructions on page 17. Trace her on to a piece of cardboard. Cut out the doll carefully with a pair of scissors.

**2** Paint the doll's face, hair, and underwear. Leave to dry.

**3** Trace around the doll to make the clothes and paint them. When you cut out the clothes make sure to leave small tags on them. These will bend behind the doll to stop them from falling off.

**4** Paint the lid of a shoe box and make two holes with a pair of scissors to support the doll. Dress up the doll in her various outfits, remembering to bend the tags behind her.

# Magic Box

*Build your own fantasy world within a box. You could choose any theme you like – a jungle, a circus, or the bottom of the sea, as here.*

**YOU WILL NEED**
paints in various shades
paintbrush
cardboard box
scissors
pictures of shells and fish
   (cut from wrapping paper)
white glue
netting
blue cellophane
cardboard
pencil
glitter
tracing and plain paper,
   for templates
sewing thread
wooden sticks

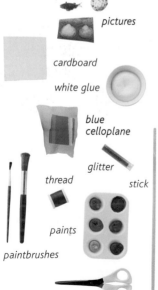

*pictures*

*cardboard*

*white glue*

*blue cellophane*

*glitter*

*thread*

*stick*

*paints*

*paintbrushes*

*scissors*

**1** Paint the cardboard box both inside and out. Allow to dry. With a pair of scissors, cut out a rectangle from the top of the box and a circle from the front.

**2** Decorate the opening with pictures of fish. Decorate the inside of the box with netting and cut-outs of shells stuck down with white glue. Glue a piece of blue cellophane to the back wall.

**3** Draw a wave on to a piece of cardboard with a pencil. Cut it out and dab on some spots of glue. Sprinkle glitter over the glue and allow to dry. Cover the wave in blue cellophane.

**4** Trace the fish and seaweed templates from the beginning of the book following the instructions on page 17. Place the templates on to a piece of cardboard and cut them out. Paint the shapes in an assortment of shades and leave to dry.

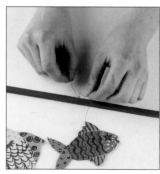

**5** Tie a piece of sewing thread to each fish and seaweed shape and tie them to wooden sticks.

## CRAFT HINT

If you can't find pictures of shells on wrapping paper, look instead in magazines for pictures. You could also draw your own if you don't find any you like.

**6** Place the sticks across the rectangle and dangle the sea-shapes inside the box.

# Little Town

*Make your own dream town out of small boxes and cardboard. Include all your preferred stores, your school and your friends' houses.*

**YOU WILL NEED**
different-sized boxes
   (matchboxes are ideal)
cardboard
scissors
white glue
paper in various shades
paints in various shades
paintbrush
toothpicks
green pom-poms
green glitter
non-hardening modelling clay
green sticky-back felt

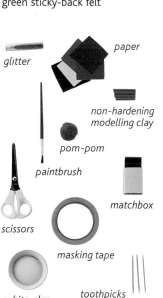

*glitter*

*paper*

*non-hardening modelling clay*

*pom-pom*

*paintbrush*

*matchbox*

*scissors*

*masking tape*

*white glue*

*toothpicks*

*paints*

**1** Remove the matches from the matchboxes and give them to an adult for safekeeping. For the roof tops of the houses, cut out square pieces of cardboard with a pair of scissors, fold them in half and stick them on to the matchboxes with white glue.

**2** Cover the houses in sheets of paper in different shades and paint on doors and windows.

**3** For the trees, paint the toothpicks brown. Glue a green pom-pom (see the project on page 82 for instructions but substitute fabric with wool (yarn)) on to a toothpick and cover it in white glue. Dab the pom-pom into a ball of green glitter and paint on red spots. To make the tree stand up, stick it into a piece of clay.

**4** For the roads, cut out strips of cardboard and paint them.

**5** Cover a large piece of cardboard with green sticky-back felt.

**6** Arrange the houses, trees and roads around the felt to create the town. If you don't glue the pieces down, you can change the position of the buildings as many times as you like and store the town away easily.

# DRESSING UP

## Salt Dough Buttons and Beads

*Make your own personalized fashion accessories.*

**YOU WILL NEED**
salt dough (see page 16)
toothpick
baking sheet
oven gloves
spatula
wire rack
paints in various shades
paintbrush
embroidery thread (floss)
rolling pin
tracing paper and cardboard, for templates
pencil
scissors
knife

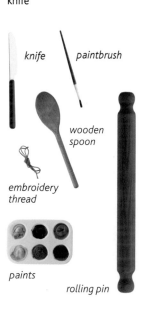

*knife*  *paintbrush*

*wooden spoon*

*embroidery thread*

*paints*

*rolling pin*

**1** Make the salt dough following the instructions on page 16. For the beads, form a small piece of salt dough on the palm of your hand to form either a round, oblong or flat shape.

**4** When the beads are completely dry, thread them on to a piece of embroidery thread.

### IMPORTANT SAFETY NOTICE
You will need an adult to help you to heat the oven and remove the salt dough once it has been baked. Use oven gloves, and do not touch the baking sheet until it has cooled.

**2** Carefully pierce a hole through the beads with a toothpick. Lay the beads out on a greased baking sheet. With the help of an adult, heat the oven to 110°C/ 225°F/ Gas 2 and put in the baking sheet. Cook for about 6 hours or until the beads are hard. Wearing oven gloves, remove the baking sheet from the oven. With a spatula slide the beads on to a wire rack. The beads will be very hot. Allow to cool before painting.

**5** For the buttons, sprinkle some flour on to a flat surface and roll out a piece of salt dough until it is 5mm (¼in) thick. Trace the templates following the instructions on page 17. Place the templates on to the dough and cut around them with a knife. Pierce four holes on each button. Bake them in the oven in the same way as the beads in step 2.

**3** Paint the beads in lots of different bright shades and patterns, such as flowers, stars, stripes, spots or anything else that you like. Allow each coat of paint to dry before adding the next so the shades don't smudge.

**6** Paint the buttons when cool and allow to dry. Sew them on to a shirt, cardigan or even a hat. You will have to remove them before washing the clothes. Salt dough should not be washed with water or in a washing machine.

# Vegetable Necklace

*Nibble away at this healthy and tasty necklace!*

**YOU WILL NEED**
chopping board
knife
carrots
celery
cabbage
skewer
string
scissors

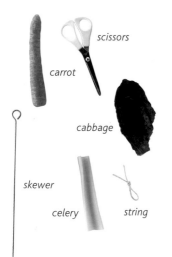

*carrot*

*scissors*

*cabbage*

*skewer*

*celery*

*string*

1 On a chopping board, use a knife to cut the carrots and celery into even chunks.

2 Cut the cabbage into triangles about the same size.

## IMPORTANT SAFETY NOTICE
You will need adult help chopping the vegetables and making holes with the skewer.

3 Carefully pierce a hole through the vegetables using a skewer.

4 Thread the vegetables on to string and cut to the correct length.

# Teddy Bear's Outfit

*Spoil your teddy with a new set of clothes.*

**YOU WILL NEED**
scissors
felt in bright shades
sewing needle
sewing thread
ribbon
white glue
paintbrush
tracing and plain paper,
    for templates
pencil
buttons
ruler
cotton fringing

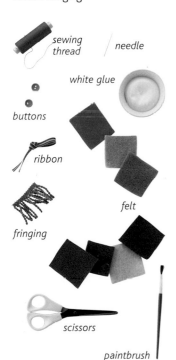

sewing thread

needle

white glue

buttons

ribbon

felt

fringing

scissors

paintbrush

**1** With a pair of scissors, carefully cut out two semi-circular pieces of bright felt to fit the width of your teddy's head. Sew the two pieces together with a needle and thread. To decorate the hat, stick on some felt shapes and some ribbon with white glue.

**2** For the waistcoat (US vest), scale-up and trace the templates from the beginning of the book following the instructions on page 17. Place the templates on to pieces of felt and cut them out carefully with scissors. Glue on some felt spots with white glue and then sew the three pieces together.

**3** Sew three buttons on to one side of the waistcoat, spacing them evenly down the side. Take care just to sew through the top layer of felt.

**4** For the scarf, cut out a 30 × 6cm (12 × 2½in) strip of felt. Glue on strips of felt for the stripes and pieces of fringing for the ends.

# Clown Face and Hat

*Put a smile on everybody's face with this happy disguise.*
*Complete the costume with the outfit on the next page.*

## YOU WILL NEED
bright fabric
scissors
sewing needle
sewing thread
2.5cm (1in) bias binding
safety pin
elastic
pom-poms in different bright
   shades or cotton wool balls
white glue
paintbrush
face paints in various shades

*white glue*
*sewing thread*
*safety pin*
*sewing needle*
*bias binding*
*elastic*
*fabric*
*pom-poms*
*paintbrush*
*scissors*

**1** To make the hat, cut out two large circles of bright fabric big enough to fit over your head, using a pair of scissors. Take a needle and thread and sew the circles together, making sure the right sides are facing and leaving a gap so that you can turn the hat right side out.

**2** Sew a piece of bias binding around the circle, 3cm (1¼in) from the edge. Attach a safety pin to the end of a length of elastic and thread it through the bias binding until it comes out of the other end. Pull the ends together until the hat is the correct size for your head. Tie a knot to secure.

**3** Stick lots of pom-poms in various shades (see the Clown's Outfit project on page 82 for instructions) or painted cotton wool balls on to the hat with some white glue and allow to dry completely before wearing. This may take a couple of hours.

**4** Ask an adult to cover your face with white face paint and paint on a big red nose and rosy cheeks. Shade in your eyebrows.

**5** Paint on a large, bright mouth around your own mouth.

**6** Draw a dark outline around your large, jolly mouth.

## IMPORTANT SAFETY NOTICE
You may need an adult's help for the sewing. When doing the face painting, make sure you use non-toxic face paints specially made to be used as make-up. Some people have a bad reaction to face paints. Try a small amount on a patch of skin before asking an adult to paint your whole face.

80

# Clown's Outfit

*This jolly outfit can be worn with the bright clown face and hat.*

**YOU WILL NEED**
cardboard
pencil
scissors
bright and patterned fabric
embroidery thread (floss)
old T-shirt in a bright shade
cotton fringing
buttons
sewing needle
sewing thread
white glue (optional)

*scissors*

*fabric*

*buttons*

*needle*

*sewing thread*

*fringing*

*T-shirt*

**1** For the pom-poms, take two pieces of cardboard and draw two circles on to them. With a pair of scissors, cut out the circles and cut out two more circles from their middles.

**2** Put the two circles together. Cut up lots of bright and patterned fabrics into strips and wrap them around the two circles.

**3** When you have almost filled in the hole you can stop wrapping the fabric strips around. Find the pieces of cardboard under all the fabric and put your scissors in between them. Cut around the fabric. Wrap a piece of embroidery thread in between the pieces of cardboard and tie a knot. Tear the cardboard away from the pom-pom and fluff it up, trimming with a pair of scissors if necessary.

**IMPORTANT SAFETY NOTICE**
You may need an adult's help for the sewing. If you prefer, you can glue all the decorations to the T-shirt, but the costume won't last as long.

**4** To make the rest of the outfit, find an old T-shirt in a bright shade and carefully sew a piece of cotton fringing around the neckline and the two sleeves.

**5** Sew the buttons around the neckline with a needle and thread.

**6** Sew on the pom-poms, or stick them on to the T-shirt with some white glue.

# Spectacular Sea-face

*Pretend you've just popped up from the ocean bed with this wonderful design of starfish and seaweed.*

**YOU WILL NEED**
face paints in various shades
tinsel wig (optional)

*face paints*

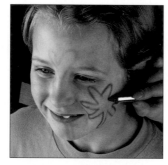

**1** Paint the outlines of the sea-shapes such as fish, seaweed and starfish on to your face.

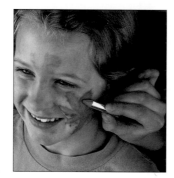

**2** Fill in the starfish and seaweed.

**3** Fill in the fish with bright shades of paint. Add a mixture of details to them.

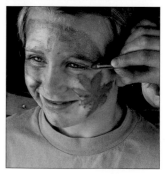

**4** Fill in around the shapes so that your face is covered with paints. Put on the tinsel wig, if using.

# Tattoo

*Wow your friends with this fake tattoo! A butterfly is shown below but you can make any design you like.*

**YOU WILL NEED**
face paints in various shades

*face paints*

**1** Paint the outline of a butterfly or your chosen design on to your arm.

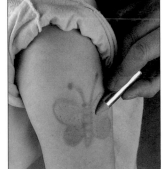

**2** Carefully begin to fill it in with your chosen shade of face paint.

**IMPORTANT SAFETY NOTICE**
To remove face paints, check the instructions on the packet. They usually come off with soap and water or baby lotion.

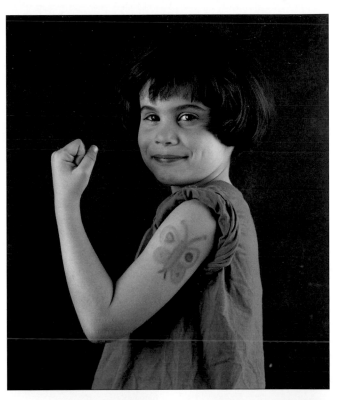

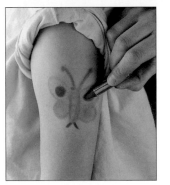

**3** Try to make your design as beautiful as possible by drawing tiny patterns and other details.

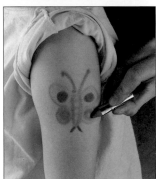

**4** Complete your design. Face paints can smudge easily, so don't let your tattoo rub against anything.

# Witch Face and Hat

*Dress up in this bewitching outfit and cast a spell!*

**YOU WILL NEED**
black paper
scissors
paintbrush
white glue
pencil
silver paper
plastic spiders (optional)
raffia
adhesive tape
black and white face paints

*plastic spider*

*silver paper*

*raffia*

*paper*

*white glue*

*paintbrush*

*adhesive tape*

*scissors*

**1** Cut out a large square of black paper with a pair of scissors. Bend it to make a cone shape big enough to fit your head, before sticking it together with white glue.

**2** Draw stars on to the silver paper and cut them out. Glue them on to the hat. If you have any plastic creepy crawlies such as spiders, glue them on to the hat as well.

**3** Attach the raffia inside the front of the hat with tape to make a fringe. Give it a trim if necessary. Make a pair of braids and attach them to the inside of the hat with tape.

**4** Shade your face white with face paints.

**5** Draw on some spooky black eyebrows and make your lips black.

**6** Draw a large spider's web on one of your cheeks and cover the rest of your face with black spots.

## IMPORTANT SAFETY NOTICE
Some people have a bad reaction to face paints. Test a small amount on a patch of skin before painting your whole face.

# Regal Crown

*Crown yourself King or Queen of the Castle!*

**YOU WILL NEED**
tape measure
cardboard
pencil
ruler
scissors
shiny paper in bright shades
ribbon
white glue
paintbrush
glitter
adhesive tape (optional)

*ruler*

*pencil*

*glitter*

*white glue*

*silver paper*

*cardboard*

*paintbrush*

*ribbon*

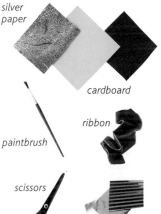

*scissors*

*shiny paper*

**1** Measure around your head with a tape measure so that you know how long to cut the cardboard band. Remember to allow a few centimetres (inches) for gluing the band together. Cut a strip of cardboard 8cm (3¼in) deep with a pair of scissors. Cover the cardboard in shiny paper and stick on a piece of ribbon with white glue.

**2** Cut out two strips of cardboard measuring 4 × 30cm (1½ × 12in) and cover them in silver paper.

**3** Make six jewel circles from shiny paper and glitter and glue them on to the ribbon.

**4** Attach the silver strips to the inside of the crown band using glue or adhesive tape. If using glue, leave to dry.

**5** Trace out five more jewel shapes from cardboard and cut them out carefully with a pair of scissors. Cover each one in gold paper and decorate with circles of shiny paper and glitter.

**6** When the jewels are dry, glue them on to the silver bands.

# Pizza Faces

*These funny faces are very easy to make. The base is a crispy crumpet topped with tomato sauce and melted cheese. The toppings are just suggestions – you can use whatever you like to create the shapes for the smiley faces.*

**YOU WILL NEED**
30ml/2 tbsp vegetable oil
1 onion, finely shredded
1 × 200g/7oz can chopped
   tomatoes
30ml/2 tbsp tomato paste
salt and ground black pepper
9 crumpets
1 × 200g/7oz packet of
   processed cheese slices
1 green (bell) pepper, seeded
   and chopped into small pieces
4–5 sliced cherry tomatoes

*crumpet*

*onion*

*tomato paste*

*cheese slices*

*chopped tomatoes*

**1** With the help of an adult, preheat the oven to 200°C/425°F/ Gas 7. Heat the oil in a large pan, add the onion and cook for about 2–3 minutes.

**2** Add the can of chopped tomatoes, tomato paste and salt and pepper to taste. Bring to a boil and cook for 5–6 minutes until the mixture becomes thick and pulpy, stirring occasionally. Remove from the heat and leave to cool. You could make this sauce in advance and keep it in the refrigerator.

**IMPORTANT SAFETY NOTICE**
Make sure an adult helps to make the sauce. Stand away from the frying pan so the hot oil doesn't splash out.

**3** Lightly toast the crumpets under a medium grill (broiler). Lay them on a baking sheet. Put a heaped teaspoonful of the tomato mixture on the top and spread it out evenly. Bake in the preheated oven for 25 minutes.

**4** Cut the cheese slices into strips and arrange them with the green pepper and the cherry tomatoes on top of the pizzas to make smiley faces. Return to the oven for about 5 minutes until the cheese melts. Serve the pizzas while still warm.

# Roly Poly Porcupines

*A meal in itself! Everyone loves frankfurter sausages and they're especially good if skewered into hot baked potatoes. Always serve with a big bowl of tomato ketchup nearby and plenty of kitchen paper.*

**YOU WILL NEED**
4 large baking potatoes
6–8 frankfurter sausages
50g/2oz cherry tomatoes
50g/2oz mild Cheddar cheese
2 sticks celery
toothpicks

**TO SERVE**
iceberg lettuce, shredded
small pieces of red (bell) pepper
    and black olive
1 carrot, chopped

celery

potato

cherry tomatoes

frankfurter sausages

Cheddar cheese

**1** With the help of an adult, preheat the oven to 200°C/400°F/Gas 6. Scrub the potatoes and prick them all over. Bake in the oven for 1–1¼ hours until soft.

**IMPORTANT SAFETY NOTICE**
You may need an adult to help chop the vegetables with a sharp knife. Make sure an adult takes the potatoes from the oven using oven gloves, and leave them to cool for a while before touching.

**2** Meanwhile, prepare the frankfurter sausages. Heat the sausages in a large pan of boiling water for 8–10 minutes until they are warmed through. Drain and leave to cool slightly.

**3** Cut the cherry tomatoes in half and when cool enough to handle, chop the sausages into 2.5cm (1in) pieces. Cut the cheese into cubes and slice the celery. Arrange them on to toothpicks.

**4** When the potatoes are cooked, remove them from the oven. Pierce the skin all over with the toothpicks topped with the frankfurters, cheese cubes, cherry tomatoes and celery slices. Serve on shredded lettuce and decorate the Porcupine's head with pieces of red pepper and olive, and a carrot snout.

# Kooky Cookies

*Easy to make and yummy to eat! Let your imagination run wild with the decorating. If it's easier, you can use tinted icing pens.*

## YOU WILL NEED

115g/4oz/1 cup self-raising (self-rising) flour
5ml/1 tsp ground ginger
5ml/1 tsp bicarbonate of soda (baking soda)
60ml/4 tbsp sugar
50g/2oz/4 tbsp softened butter
25g/2 tbsp golden syrup (light corn syrup)

## ICING

115g/4oz/½ cup softened butter
250g/8oz/2 cups icing (confectioners') sugar, sifted
5ml/1 tsp lemon juice
a few drops of food dye (optional)
icing pens in various shades
bright confectionery

sugar

flour

butter

golden syrup

ginger

icing sugar

**1** Sift the flour, ginger and bicarbonate of soda into a large mixing bowl. Add the sugar, then rub in the butter with your fingertips until the mixture resembles fine breadcrumbs.

**2** Add the golden syrup and mix to a dough. Preheat the oven to 190°C/375°F/Gas 5.

**3** Roll out to 3mm (⅛in) thick on a lightly-floured surface. Stamp out the shapes with cookie cutters and transfer to a lightly greased baking sheet. Bake for 5–10 minutes before transferring to a wire rack to cool.

**4** To make the icing, beat the butter in a bowl with a wooden spoon until it is light and fluffy. Add the sifted icing sugar to the butter a little at a time and continue beating. Add lemon juice and food dye (if using).

**5** Spread the icing over the cooled cookies and leave to set.

**6** When the icing has set, make patterns on the icing with a range of vibrant icing pens and decorate with bright confectionery.

# Jolly Orange Boats

*These are so easy to make and fun to eat. The only difficult thing is waiting for the jelly to set! These boats make a yummy dessert or party treat. You could serve with ice cream for something extra special.*

**YOU WILL NEED**
2 oranges
1 packet orange-flavoured jelly
4 sheets rice paper or
    edible paper
toothpicks

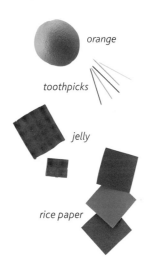

orange

toothpicks

jelly

rice paper

## IMPORTANT SAFETY NOTICE
You may need an adult's help cutting the oranges. Be very careful whenever you handle knives.

**1** Cut the oranges in half lengthways. Scrape out the flesh, taking care not to pierce the skins. Chop up the flesh.

**2** Make the jelly according to the packet instructions. Add the orange flesh while the jelly cools.

**3** Place the orange shells on to a baking sheet and pour in the jelly mixture. Leave for 1 hour to set. Once set, cut the skins in half again using a knife to create little boats.

**4** Cut the rice paper or edible paper sheets into eight squares. Pierce each corner with a toothpick and attach the sail to the middle of the orange boat.

# Chocolate Witchy Apples

*These chocolate witches are great fun to make and eat. Be careful with the melted chocolate, though, as it has a nasty habit of getting everywhere!*

**YOU WILL NEED**
6 small eating apples
6 wooden sticks
250g/8oz milk chocolate
6 ice cream cones
confectionery, for decorating

*apple*

*milk chocolate*

*confectionery*

*wooden stick*

*ice cream cone*

**1** Peel and thoroughly dry the apples. Press a wooden stick into the core of each one.

**2** Put the chocolate in a heatproof bowl and place In the microwave or over a pan of simmering water, and gently melt it.

**IMPORTANT SAFETY NOTICE**
Melted chocolate is very hot! Make sure an adult helps you melt it.

**3** When the chocolate has melted, tilt the pan and dip the apple into it, coating it well. Place the coated apple on a baking sheet lined with baking parchment.

**4** Holding the stick, use a little melted chocolate to attach the cone for a hat. The cone can also be decorated by sticking confectionery on with spare melted chocolate. Repeat with the other five apples.

# INDEX